GLIMPSES OF ISLAMIC HISTORY

General Editor: Ashraf Abu Turab

ABU BAKR
THE FIRST CALIPH

Adapted from Arabic by
Dr. Muhammad Rashid Feroze

THE ISLAMIC FOUNDATION

© The Islamic Foundation 1976/1396 A.H.
Reprinted 1979/1399 A.H., 1982/1402 A.H., 1986/1406 A.H. and 1994/1415 A.H.

ISBN 0 9503954 4 7

This biography of Caliph Abu Bakr is based upon Sabir Abduh Ibrahim's book *Abu Bakr,* published by Maktaba al-Manar al-Islamia, P.O. Box 633, Kuwait.

Published by
The Islamic Foundation
Markfield Dawah Centre
Ratby Lane, Markfield
Leicester LE67 9RN, UK

Quran House, PO Box 30611,
Nairobi, Kenya

PMB 3193,
Kano, Nigeria

Printed by
JOSEPH A. BALL (Printers) LTD., Leicester

2

FOREWORD

Reading material developed on graded lines related to Islam, its history and its outstanding people, is hard to find in the English language. Yet the growing generation of young Muslim people is looking for a series of readers which would give them a taste of the glorious heritage of Islam. The reading of graded readers serves to instil in the young a sense of attachment to the Islamic way of life.

"Abu Bakr—The First Caliph"—the first of the 'Glimpses of Islamic History' series—is an attempt to meet this need of essential books written by Muslims for young people.

This book tries to catch some of the spirit of the times by bringing into focus the personalities involved. Abu Bakr was the most dedicated companion of the Prophet Muhammad (peace be upon him). This book tells of the great personal sacrifices made by Abu Bakr and how he was elected to the office of the Caliphate by the populace after the death of the Prophet. The latter part of the book tells with what great insight he overcame the initial difficulties and disrupted the forces of evil which were fighting tooth and nail to arrest the tide of Islamic movement. The last chapter is a tribute to his great organisational and administrative talents with which he served the Islamic state and built it with great care and caution.

Now a word about the Islamic Foundation—the producers of the present series.

The Islamic Foundation is a research and educational organisation. It has been founded to improve human communication and develop a better understanding of Islam to Muslims and non-Muslims alike. It is producing literature on Islam in the major languages of the world.

The Islamic Foundation proposes to produce a graded series of readers and other educational material to cater for the needs of Islamic education at different levels. For beginners, it has published The Children's Book of Islam. It will appear in several other parts. These books are to be followed by a series on *Essentials of Islam,* a course of some forty lessons on the basic teachings of Islam.

Many people have helped us by their comments and suggestions during the course of translating and producing this book and it would take too much space to thank them all individually. I am indebted to Dr. Muhammad Rashid Feroze, who took the trouble of adapting the Arabic text into English. Special thanks are due to Mrs. Daphne Buckmaster for her courtesy in revising the manuscript. Mr. Sultan Farooqui deserves special mention for the great care with which he made the book presentable with its impressive art work.

A.A.T.

CONTENTS

Pages

1

THE FRIEND

The caravan had completed its trade dealings in Syria and was resting before making the return journey to Makka. A traveller with the caravan, Abu Bakr, had had a dream which puzzled him, so he went to see an old man who, on hearing the story, raised his head and said: "Listen to me; if Allah makes your dream come true, then indeed He will raise a Prophet from your people. And you will be his helper in life and successor after his death." Abu Bakr became quiet on hearing this and, shaking his head in wonder and awe, returned to his tent in peace and tranquility.

After a few days, the caravan proceeded on its way to Makka, having enjoyed a very successful and profitable journey to Syria. On the journey, the days sometimes passed quickly and sometimes slowly. Abu Bakr remembered his strange dream from time to time and wondered at the old man's interpretation of it. He decided to wait for the appearance of the Prophet mentioned by the old man.

At about this time, the Prophet Muhammad (peace be upon him) began his mission as commanded by Allah. He invited the people to believe in the Oneness of Allah, the Lord of creation and explained to them why their current beliefs and actions were wrong.

Abu Bakr was a close friend of the Prophet Muhammad (peace be upon him) and they had both visited Syria with the caravans. Their conversations have been reported in many sayings of the Prophet (peace be upon him) and his Companions.

When Abu Bakr returned to Makka, the people told him that his friend, the Prophet Muhammad (peace be upon him) was suffering from madness. They asked him to talk to his friend and prevent him from insulting and abusing their gods. When they met, they sat down to have a heart-to-heart talk. They had exchanged only a few words when Abu Bakr declared his

The Middle East during the Life of the Prophet Muhammad

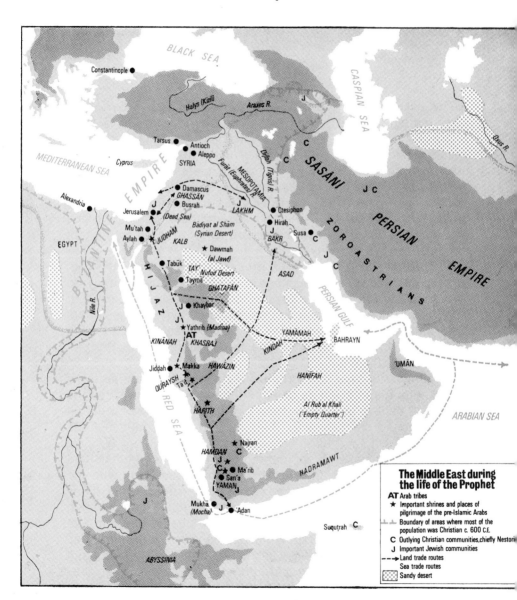

The Middle East during the life of the Prophet

AT Arab tribes
★ Important shrines and places of pilgrimage of the pre-Islamic Arabs
⊥⊥ Boundary of areas where most of the population was Christian c. 600 C.E.
C Outlying Christian communities, chiefly Nestorii
J Important Jewish communities
– – – Land trade routes
Sea trade routes
▦ Sandy desert

firm and unshakable belief in his friend and his religious teachings. He, therefore, became the first person to believe in the call to Allah's faith.

Abu Bakr's conversion to Islam remained a secret except to a few people. But he became a great supporter of Islam, and his faith was strengthened rapidly. He made up his mind to spread the teachings of Islam among the leaders and elders of the *Quraysh*, the noblest tribe of Arabia, without fearing the results. until the Prophet (peace be upon him) agreed.

He became a great friend of the Prophet of Islam (peace be upon him) and requested him to start preaching Islam openly, but the Prophet (peace be upon him) did not agree, saying the moment was not ripe. Abu Bakr repeated his request daily.

They went as a group to the *Ka'ba*, where the elders of the *Quraysh* sat talking among themselves. They approached the elders and sat down near them. Then Abu Bakr stood up and addressed the people. He invited them to believe in the Almighty Allah who is Unique and has no partner, and to worship and obey Him alone. The Prophet Muhammad (peace be upon him) sat down listening to the speech. Unfortunately, the early historians of Islam have not reported the text of this first speech. They have only mentioned the following few words: "He stood up to address the people, and the Prophet (peace be upon him) was sitting and listening." Thus he was the first preacher who invited the people to believe in Allah and His Prophet (peace be upon him).

The speech delivered by Abu Bakr was a stern warning to the elders of the *Quraysh* and their leaders. When they saw him delivering the speech, they attacked him and the small group of Muslims. Utba bin Rabi'a took off his shoes, and struck Abu Bakr's face until it started to bleed. The fight between the two parties continued until the arrival of the Banu Tamim, the tribe to which Abu Bakr belonged. They chased the idol worshippers away from Abu Bakr and carried him to his home. They thought that he was dead.

Four members of the Banu Tamim wrapped Abu Bakr in a mantle and carried him to his house, where they put him on one of the wooden beds. Then they returned to the *Ka'ba* to swear that they would slay Utba bin Rabi'a if Abu Bakr died.

MAKKA

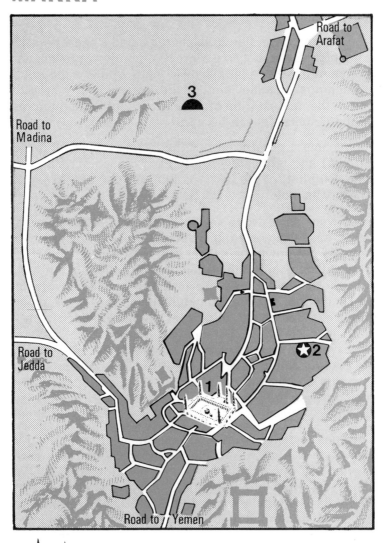

1. Masjid Al-Haram
2. The House in which Muhammad was born
3. Tomb of Khadija

Ummul Khayr Salma, her heart beating fast, looked at her son and called him saying "Atiq ... Atiq." But she could not hear anything except the echo of her own voice. She called him again: "O Abdullah! O Abu Bakr!" But Abu Bakr was in a deep coma.

His old father came and struck his stick in a distant corner of the house. His wife Salma went to welcome him. She said to him: "O Abu Qahafa! This is Atiq! (the nickname of Abu Bakr). Four persons of the Banu Tamim have brought him to me. He seems to be almost dead." The man and his wife sat around Abu Bakr. His mother washed his face with water, and she sat near him massaging his hands and feet until sunset.

Abu Bakr made a little movement. Then he opened his eyes and said in a clear tone: "How is the Prophet of Allah (peace be upon him)". His mother spoke to him with some relief: "How are you Abu Bakr?" He replied: "How is the Prophet of Allah (peace be upon him)?" She said: "I do not know, my son."

"Go to Fatima bint al-Khattab and ask her about him", he requested. His mother stood up and went immediately to the house of Fatima. She found her there and said: "Abu Bakr has been badly hurt. Utba has beaten him at the Ka'ba. He is very anxious to know how Muhammad bin Abdullah is."

"I do not know what happended to the Prophet of Allah but I can go with you to Abu Bakr if you wish."

Both the women went to Abu Bakr and when Fatima sat near him, he asked her: "How is the Prophet of Allah?"

"The Prophet of Allah is in the house of Ibn al-Arqam", was all she could tell him. Fatima then pointed out that his mother was there, saying in a clear voice: "Do you know? Your mother is here."

Salma then came to her son with a cup of milk and said to him: "Take it and drink it, my son, so that you may have a little strength."

"By Allah I shall not taste any food or drink until I meet the Prophet of Allah!"

They waited together until one third of the night was over. The two women supported Abu Bakr so that he could stand and walk. He leaned on the right hand of his mother Salma and on the left hand of Fatima bint al-Khattab, his sister in Islam.

They walked slowly until they reached the house of Ibn al-Arqam. As soon as they entered the house, Abu Bakr went to the room of the Prophet of Allah (peace be upon him) and greeted him: "This is Abu Bakr, O Prophet of Allah." The Prophet of Allah (peace be upon him) stood up to welcome him with a smile and asked him: "How are you, Abu Bakr?"

"O Prophet of Allah! Nothing has happened to me except for an injury on my face caused by the evil doer." The Prophet (peace be upon him) then prayed for his welfare and recovery. Abu Bakr then made a request to the Prophet (peace be upon him): "This is my mother. Invite her to believe in Allah, and pray to Allah for her so that He may save her from Hell Fire."

The Prophet (peace be upon him) then asked Salma to have faith in Allah. And hardly a few minutes had passed when Salma declared: "I am a witness to the fact that there is no true God except Allah and Muhammad is the Prophet of Allah." Abu Bakr was happy to see that his mother had accepted Islam. Thus Abu Bakr was the first man among his people to respond to the call of Allah's faith, the first to raise his voice for the propagation of the faith in Allah and His Prophet (peace be upon him) and also the first person to have his faith in Allah tested.

Before entering the fold of Islam, Abu Bakr was loved by his people. He had avoided all the bad habits then prevalent among the Arabs. He claimed that he did not drink alcohol before or after embracing Islam, and that he never worshipped an idol. He says: "I never prostrated myself before an idol. When I reached the age of puberty, Abu Qahafa (my father) caught me by the hand and went along with me to a temple where idols were kept. He said to me: "This is your goddess". He left me there and went away. I went to the idol and said: 'I am hungry. Give me food!' It did not answer. Then I said: 'I am naked. Give me clothes'. It did not respond. Then I threw a stone at it hitting its mouth."

We do not know any Companion of the Prophet (peace be upon him) who never worshipped an idol, except Abu Bakr. His action was only through Allah's help and guidance.

During the days of *Jahiliyyah* (ignorance)—the period before the advent of Islam—Abu Bakr, being a kind and noble man, was appointed as a representative of the people of the *Quraysh* for cases of ransom and penalty. He collected camels, goods and other property whenever some incident happened which required some payment by a member of the *Quraysh* tribe. He also made payments on their behalf, and they accepted his decisions wholeheartedly. Their reliance on him was ample proof of his honesty. He was held in great regard in the days of Islam and made the noble Companions follow his opinion. Among them were Sa'd bin Abi Waqqas, Abdur Rahman bin Awf, Talha bin Ubaydullah, Zubayr Ibn al-Awam and Abu Ubayda Ibn al-Jarrah. Abu Bakr also had the best knowledge of family tree of the Arab tribes and their leading chiefs and for this reason was called "the scholar of the *Quraysh*."

Besides possessing all these qualities, Abu Bakr was a rich tradesman. His capital was forty thousand *dirhams**, which he spent entirely in the cause of Islam. We shall see later in this book what a great influence Abu Bakr's wealth had in the spread of Islam among the people. Many slaves of the tribes entered the fold of Islam after they had been freed from their harsh masters with the money provided by Abu Bakr.

Abu Bakr freed seven *Mawali* (wards of tribes) and slaves whom he had bought with his money. Among them was Bilal bin Rabah, the *muezzin*** of the Prophet (peace be upon him) whom he had bought for five ounces of gold from Umayya bin Khalaf. He had also bought Zanira, the blind woman from Syria and freed her. The people of *Quraysh* said of her: "None will give back her sight except—the gods—*Lat* and *Uzza*", She replied: "By Allah, that is not true. *Lat* and *Uzza* do not know who worships them. My Lord is able to restore my sight."

And Allah accepted her prayer and restored her sight. The people of *Quraysh* said on this occasion: "This is the magic of Muhammad."

Abu Bakr had also freed a woman called al-Nahdiya. She and her daughter were living in the custody of a non-Muslim woman of *Bani Abd al-Dar.* Once she sent both of them to her corn-grinder. And she was saying: "By Allah I shall never free either of you!"

Fortunately, Abu Bakr was passing that way, and he heard

---

*The *dirham* was a silver coin of Arabia. The coin is still used in some countries.

**One who calls Muslims to prayer.

her words. He said to her: "Do you want to get rid of your slaves?"

She replied: "You have spoiled them. I shall free both of them."

He enquired: "How much for both of them?" Abu Bakr paid the amount demanded, and then he addressed them; "Both of you are free. Return her corn to her."

One of them said: "Let us finish our job, O Abu Bakr, and then we shall return it."

He replied: "As you like."

One day Abu Bakr came across a slave woman who was being beaten by her master. Abu Bakr bought her and freed her immediately. He also freed a number of other slaves.

Thus Abu Bakr spent the money which he had earned from his business on these *Mawali* and slaves so that they could embrace the faith of Islam—a faith in which he believed firmly. He dedicated his life and possessions to the spread of Islam, so that it might reach out and be heard in all parts of the world.

Abu Bakr spent his life and property in the struggle for the cause of Islam, in particular, helping those people whose lives and souls were pledged to Allah. He did not spare his life or possessions in following Allah's faith. He rather presented them voluntarily for the purification of his soul.

There is no doubt that the money spent by Abu Bakr for the cause of Islam played a major role in the propagation of the faith in its early stages. The Qur'an acknowledges the role of money and personal effort and sacrifice in the cause of Allah: "Those people who believed, migrated and struggled in the way of Allah with their possessions and lives have a great position in the eyes of Allah. And they are the successful."

2

THE COMPANION

Abu Bakr stayed with the Prophet (peace be upon him) in Makka until the *Quraysh* stepped up their campaign against the Muslim community. The Prophet of Allah (peace be upon him) then allowed his Companions to emigrate to Ethiopia. Abu Bakr went to the Prophet (peace be upon him) to ask his permission to emigrate along with the others. The permission was given. Abu Bakr then mounted his camel and started on the rough journey. After a journey of one or two days from Makka, he reached a place called Bark al-Ghammad where he met Ibn al-Daghna, the chief of a tribe. He asked with an air of surprise: "Where are you going, Abu Bakr?"

Abu Bakr replied: "My people have expelled me, troubled me and made life miserable for me. So I want to travel in the world and to worship and obey my Lord."

"No! By Allah, you are the glory of the tribe. You help the strangers and do good deeds. O Abu Bakr, a man like you cannot be found easily. Go back, and you shall be under my protection. Worship your Lord in your own land!"

So Abu Bakr returned with him, and when they entered Makka, Ibn al-Daghna went towards the *Ka'ba*. He spoke loudly to the chiefs of the tribe sitting in the courtyard of the shrine: "O people of *Quraysh*!" I have given protection to Abu Bakr Ibn Abi Qahafa. Now nobody should approach him except with good intentions."

Days passed and nobody approached Abu Bakr for any good or evil purpose. Abu Bakr used to offer his prayers in a place near his house. He was a man of tender heart and was extremely sensitive. Whenever he stood up to recite the Qur'an, he wept and made others cry. Tears rolled down his cheeks as a result of the recitation. A large number of children, servants and women stood behind him in prayer.

They looked at him and wondered at his expression and

MADINA

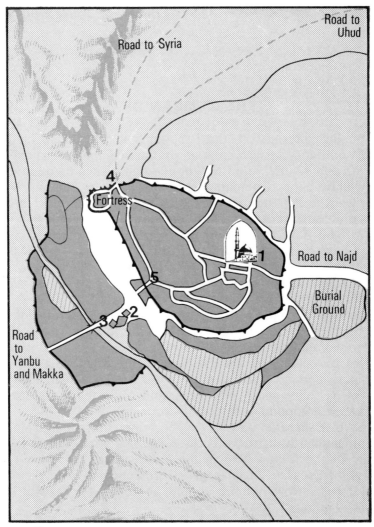

1. MASJID AN-NABAWI
   or the Prophet's Mosque
2. The Prophet's Musalla or Prayer-place
3. The Mosque of Umar
4. The Syrian Gate   5. The Egyptian Gate

16

movements. Some elders of the *Quraysh* were afraid of the influence of Abu Bakr's prayers on these children and servants.

They appealed to Ibn al-Daghna: "O Ibn al-Daghna! You have not protected this man so that he may trouble us. Whenever he prays and recites what Muhammad has claimed to have been revealed to him, he cries aloud. We are afraid that our children, women and old people will be led astray. Go and ask him to stay in his house where he can do what he likes."

Ibn al-Daghna went to Abu Bakr and said: "O Abu Bakr, I have not protected you with the purpose that you may trouble other people. They do not accept your position and that is why they feel troubled by you. Go to your house, and there do what you like."

When Abu Bakr heard Ibn al-Daghna ordering him to pray in his house, he looked pained. He felt that Ibn al-Daghna was wilfully controlling his freedom of belief and worship. He realised that protection by Ibn al-Daghna or any other person was not fitting to his position as a believer with a strong faith, and that Allah's protection was stronger and more everlasting than that of Ibn al-Daghna or others like him. He addressed him: "Shall I relinquish your protection?"

Ibn al-Daghna replied: "yes, relinquish my protection".

Abu Bakr answered: "I relinquish it".

Ibn al-Daghna went to the *Ka'ba* and announced: "O people of *Quraysh*! Abu Bakr bin Abi Qahafa has relinquished my protection. Your enemy is with you!"

Abu Bakr stood up for a moment and then began walking towards the *Ka'ba*. On his way, he met one of the notorious characters of the *Quraysh,* who threw a handful of dust at his head. By chance, al-'As bin Wa'il passed by Abu Bakr at that moment. Abu Bakr said to him: "Don't you see what this fellow has done?" al-'As answered: "Have you not brought it on yourself O Abu Bakr?"

Abu Bakr replied quietly, as if he were talking to himself: "O Lord."

The call to Allah's faith spread among the people with greater intensity as time went on. People from *Yathrib* (Madina) embraced Islam, and gave their pledge to the Prophet (peace be upon him) that they would give him full protection with their lives and possessions, and would spend their lives and blood in the cause of Allah and the propagation of Islam. The Prophet (peace be upon him) saw the hardships of his Companions and ordered them to go to *Yathrib* and live there with their brothers in Islam until Allah improved their circumstances. Abu Bakr went to see the Prophet (peace be upon him) and to seek permission to travel to *Yathrib*. The Prophet (peace be upon him), however, did not allow him to travel and said: "Don't be in a hurry. Perhaps Allah may provide you with a companion."

Abu Bakr became quiet, and he requested that the Prophet of Allah (peace be upon him) might be his companion. Abu Bakr bought two camels for eight hundred *dirhams*. He kept them at his house in order to feed and prepare them for the journey along with his companion, the Prophet (peace be upon him).

Allah ordered His Prophet (peace be upon him) to migrate on the day the *Quraysh* had planned to assassinate him. The Prophet (peace be upon him), therefore, visited the house of Abu Bakr soon after midday. Abu Bakr was surprised by the arrival of the Prophet (peace be upon him) because it was not his habit to come at that time. He usually came in the morning or in the evening. Abu Bakr welcomed the Prophet (peace be upon him) cordially, and requested him to sit on his divan. After a few moments rest, the Prophet (peace be upon him) said to Abu Bakr: "Come, let us go!"

Abu Bakr replied: "O Prophet of Allah, here are my two daughters, that is all that I have."

"Allah has ordered me to leave home and migrate", the Prophet (peace be upon him) told Abu Bakr.

Abu Bakr cried with joy: "Companionship, O Prophet of Allah!"

After a while, Abu Bakr said: "O Prophet of Allah! Here are the two camels which I was preparing for this day."

Both of them waited until the approach of evening, and when it became quite dark, they went out of an opening in the wall, and headed towards the cave known as *Ghar-i-Thawr,* in the hills near Makka. Both of them entered the cave. Abu Bakr had instructed his son Abdullah to listen to the talk of the town during the day about them and report to them at nightfall any new scheme of the *Quraysh.* Abu Bakr sometimes went ahead of the Prophet (peace be upon him) and sometimes behind him on his way to the cave. When the Prophet (peace be upon him) asked him the reason for this action, Abu Bakr said: "When I am behind you, I am afraid that you will be attacked from the front, and when I am in front, I am afraid that you will be attacked from behind."

When they stood together at the entrance to a cave, and the Prophet (peace be upon him) wanted to enter, Abu Bakr went in first, saying, "By Allah! Do not enter before me, so that if there is anything in it, it may harm me instead of harming you."

Abu Bakr entered the cave and searched it on all sides. He found a big hole which he covered with his bed-sheet. He covered two other holes near the big one with both his feet in order to stop any harmful insects. Then the Prophet (peace be upon him) entered the cave, and he was very tired. He put his head on the lap of Abu Bakr and went to sleep.

Unfortunately, there was a large snake in one of the two holes, and it bit the foot of Abu Bakr. He cried and tears fell from his eyes onto the face of the Prophet (peace be upon him) who was awakened and asked: "What has happened to you, Abu Bakr?"

He replied: "I have been bitten."

The Prophet (peace be upon him) rubbed his fingers over Abu Bakr's foot, praying to Allah for his recovery, and immediately Abu Bakr felt better. The Prophet (peace be upon him) then prayed: "O Allah. Bless Abu Bakr on the Day of Judgement!"

Some people of the *Quraysh* were searching for the Prophet (peace be upon him) and stopped at the entrance of the cave. Abu Bakr was frightened about the safety of the Prophet, (peace be upon him) and he said: "O Prophet of Allah, if any of them looks at his feet, he will see us!"

The Prophet (peace be upon him) answered: "You think only of the two of us, but Allah is the third here. Don't worry, Allah is with us!"

Allah blurred the vision of those people and they could not see the Prophet (peace be upon him) and his Companion. They returned quietly to Makka. Then the two refugees came out of the cave after staying there for three days and began their journey to Madina.

It is worth mentioning here that Abu Bakr carried all his money, amounting to six thousand *dirhams,* on him when he left Makka, in the company of the Prophet (peace be upon him) for Madina. But the question arises here as to how Abu Bakr's capital was reduced in thirteen years from forty thousand *dirhams* to six thousand. The answer is that he had spent all his money in the way of Allah. Abu Bakr's daughter Asma has reported the following interesting story.

"When the Prophet of Allah left Makka, Abu Bakr accompanied him with all his money. It was five thousand *dirhams.* My grandfather Abu Qahafa, who came to visit us, was blind and said: "By Allah, I think he has left you in trouble, taking away all his money'. I said: 'No Grandpa, he has left a lot of money for us'. Then I took a few pieces of stone and put them in a pit in our house, where my father used to keep his money. I covered it with a piece of cloth. Then I caught the hand of my grandfather, and said to him: 'Grandpa, put your hand on this money. He put his hand on it and then said: 'I don't worry if he has left this money for you. He has done well. This is your share.' And Asma said: "By Allah, my father did not leave anything for us. But I wanted to keep the grandpa quiet."

Thus Asma, the daughter of Abu Bakr, was a believer with a strong love for the Prophet of Allah (peace be upon him), and the entire family of Abu Bakr shared his love. Historians believe that except for the family of Abu Bakr, no other Companion's family is known to have four generations as the Companions of the Prophet (peace be upon him). In the family of Abu Bakr, four generations became Companions of the Prophet (peace be upon him)—Abu Atiq, his father Abdur Rahman, his grandfather Abu Bakr, and his great-grandfather Abu Qahafa.

This story of the migration to Madina shows the greatness of Abu Bakr. It indicates the great love that Abu Bakr had for the Prophet (peace be upon him), and his sacrifice of his life and property for the cause of Islam. He dedicated his life and property to protect the life of the Prophet (peace be upon him). Hassan bin Thabit, the famous poet, one day praised Abu Bakr before the Prophet (peace be upon him) by reciting a poem:

The two great persons were in a cave,
And the enemy went around and climbed the mount,
And they knew his love for the Prophet of Allah,
None else from the people could equal him on this count.

The Prophet (peace be upon him) laughed and said: "You are right, Hassan. That is a fact." The Prophet of Allah then declared: "If I were to choose a best friend from among the people, I would choose Abu Bakr."

The Prophet (peace be upon him) reached Madina. And the people of Madina gave him a rousing welcome. The Prophet of

Allah (peace be upon him) then set up the relationship of brotherhood between the immigrants and the local Muslims. He made Abu Bakr a brother of Kharija bin Zayd.

Some of the Companions of the Prophet (peace be upon him) began to debate with the Jews and Christians, and urged them to believe in the Prophethood of Muhammad (peace be upon him). One day Abu Bakr went to a meeting of the Jewish people. He found there Fanhas, a Jewish Rabbi. Abu Bakr said to him: "Think of your faith, Fanhas! Fear Allah and embrace Islam! By Allah, you know that Muhammad is the Prophet of Allah. He has come to you with the true mission from Him."

Fanhas gave a discourteous reply, full of conceit and rancour, to Abu Bakr. He said: "O Abu Bakr, by Allah, we don't need your Allah; indeed He needs us. We don't make humble requests to Him; He humbly requests us. We are rich in comparison to Him. He is not rich in comparison to us. If He had been richer than we are, He would not ask us for a loan of our money, as your friend thinks. He forbids interest on money to you, but He gives us interest. If He had been richer than we are, He would not give interest to us. And He refers to this point in His verse: "Whosoever gives Allah a good loan, He will give a large interest on it" (Qur'an).

Abu Bakr became angry listening to the words of disrespect for Allah. He raised his hand and slapped Fanhas.

Fanhas got up and went to see the Prophet (peace be upon him) and he complained to him about Abu Bakr's behaviour. The Prophet (peace be upon him) asked Abu Bakr: "What was the reason behind your action?"

Abu Bakr replied: "O Prophet of Allah! The enemy of Allah said something very shocking. He thinks that Allah is poor and that they are rich in comparison to Him. When he said this, I became angry for the sake of Allah, and gave him a thrashing".

Fanhas denied what Abu Bakr had said. But Allah revealed some verses (of the Qur'an) supporting the statement of Abu Bakr, and condemning Fanhas severely: "Allah has heard the statement of the people who said: 'Indeed Allah is poor, and we are rich'. We shall write what they have said, and their slaying of Prophets without justification. And We shall say: 'Taste the punishment of Hell Fire.' This will be for what they have done. And Allah does not do any injustice to His servants,"—Qur'an.

Time passed on, and the Muslims increased in number and

strength until the second year of the *Hijra* which means the migration of the Prophet from Makka to Madina.

The Battle of *Badr,* one of the earliest battles in the history of Islam, occurred in that year. The Prophet (peace be upon him) stood up during that battle and prayed to Allah: "O Allah! Grant unto me what You have promised. Oh Lord, if You allow this group of Muslims to perish, You will never be worshipped on the earth."

He kept on praying, until his mantle fell from his shoulders. Abu Bakr came, and replaced the sheet on his shoulders, and said: "O Prophet of Allah! Your devotion to your Lord is sufficient for us. He will indeed give you what He has promised."

When the two armies were about to meet each other in battle, Sa'd bin Muaz came to the Prophet (peace be upon him) and said: "O Prophet of Allah! Should we not make a special chair for you so that you may sit in it, and we can be around you as and when required? And we can meet the enemy. And if Allah gives us support and victory over our enemies, that is what we desire. Otherwise, we shall sit near you and meet the non-Muslims." The Prophet (peace be upon him) agreed with him.

When the special chair was made, the Companions consulted among themselves as to who would remain on duty with the Prophet (peace be upon him) to protect him against the attacks of the disbelievers. None of the other Companions came forward to accept this duty because of the seriousness of the position and its importance. But Abu Bakr alone came forward to protect the Prophet (peace be upon him). He waved his sword over the head of the Prophet (peace be upon him) and sat with him throughout the battle and challenged everyone who tried to come near him. He proved to be the bravest and strongest man in his duty on that day. Ali bin Abi Talib said of him: "Abu Bakr is the bravest of all."

On that day, Abu Bakr challenged his son Abdur Rahman, who was still a disbeliever, to come forward to fight. But the young man kept away from his father. Sometime later, after embracing Islam, Abdur Rahman told his father: "Father, you had become my target on the day of the battle of *Badr,* but I did justice to you and did not slay you!"

Abu Bakr replied: "If you had been my target, I would not have forgiven you!"

Thus Abu Bakr was a man who knew no limits in his fight against the disbelievers, even against his son, his own flesh.

The Ka'ba—The 'House of Allah' at Makka.

And he maintained his campaign in the cause of Allah's faith. Abu Bakr participated similarly in the Battle of *Uhud* and other battles against the disbelievers under the command of the Prophet (peace be upon him), and he never showed any reluctance. He stayed with the Prophet (peace be upon him) in Madina until the eighth year of the *Hijra,* when Makka was conquered, and then he entered the *Ka'ba.* Abu Bakr returned home to get his father, and brought him to the Prophet (peace be upon him). When the Prophet (peace be upon him) saw him, he said to Abu Bakr: "Why did you not leave the old man in his home, so that I could come to meet him?"

Abu Bakr answered: "O Prophet of Allah, it is better for him to come to you than for you to go to him." The Prophet (peace be upon him) then spoke to Abu Qahafa, and he embraced Islam, and proved to be a good Muslim.

Later on, the Prophet (peace be upon him) appointed Abu Bakr the leader of the *Hajj* (pilgrimage to Makka) in the ninth year of the *Hijra.* The Prophet (peace be upon him) then performed his last *Hajj* known as *Hajjatul Wida.* After the pilgrimage was over, the Prophet of Allah (peace be upon him) fell ill. Several days later the Prophet (peace be upon him) went to the mosque with his head wrapped up. However, he only looked through the doors of the mosque, as he was too weak to enter. In those days, the houses of the Companions were built around the mosque, their compounds forming the walls of the mosque. Then the Prophet said: "Look at those doors adjoining the mosque. Close all of them except the one belonging to the house of Abu Bakr, because I do not know of any of my Companions more worthy of respect than him." This saying of the Prophet (peace be upon him) was proof of the fact that Abu Bakr ranked first among his Companions, who numbered one hundred and twenty thousand at the time, according to one estimate.

The Prophet (peace be upon him) returned to his house, and his illness became acute. When the Prophet (peace be upon him) grew very weak and the time for prayers came, he said to Bilal (the *Muezzin* of the Prophet's mosque): "Ask Abu Bakr to lead the prayers."

Bilal looked for Abu Bakr, but could not find him. He then asked Umar Ibn al-Khattab to lead the prayers and when Umar said "Allah Akbar", the Prophet (peace be upon him) heard his voice. He asked: "Where is Abu Bakr? Allah and the Muslims want him!" Abu Bakr was then called to lead the prayers, and he came and led the prayers. The Prophet's health then improved for a while and Abu Bakr went to him and said: "O Prophet of Allah! I see that you are in good health by the grace of Allah and to our great joy and happiness." Then he asked for permission to return home to see his family and he was allowed to do so.

During the day, when Abu Bakr was sitting in the company of his family, the tragic news about the death of the Prophet (peace be upon him) was brought to him. He went quickly to the house of 'Ayesha, and found the Prophet of Allah (peace be upon him) lying in a corner with a sheet over his body.

al- Masjid an-Nabawi—The Prophet's Mosque at Madina.

He leaned over him, removed the cover from his face, and kissed him farewell, saying: "You have tasted the death destined for you by Allah, but you will never have death afflict you after this!"

He then put the cover on his face and went outside. He saw the people assembled outside the mosque, and Umar Ibn al-Khattab was addressing them: "O people! The Prophet of Allah (peace be upon him) has not died. He has gone to his Lord, just as Musa (Moses), the son of Imran, has gone."

Abu Bakr interrupted him and said: "O Umar, be silent."

Then he addressed the people: "O people! Whoever worshipped Muhammad should know that Muhammad is dead. Whoever worshipped Allah should know that Allah is alive and will never die."

Then he read the following verse from the Qur'an:

"Muhammad is naught but a Prophet. The other Prophets have gone before him. If he died or were killed, will you then turn on your backs? And whosoever turns on his back shall not harm Allah at all. Indeed, Allah will reward the grateful believers".

The people then cried, and went away, with their eyes full of tears and their hearts full of grief.

3

THE CALIPH

A man approached Abu Bakr and Umar when they were standing and talking to the people, and said to them: "The Ansars (the supporters of the Prophet from Madina) have gathered in the house of Bani Sa'ida."

Abu Bakr then said to Umar: "Let us go to our Ansar brothers, and hear what they are saying".

The two men went together, followed by a large number of Muhajirin (the immigrants from Makka). Abu Ubayda also joined them, and they eventually reached the house known as Saqifa Bani Sa'ida. Then they saw a man from the Ansars who was saying: "We are the supporters of Allah, and the standard-bearers of Islam. O immigrants! You are living here among us under our protection. Now a group of your people wants to uproot us and have the upper hand."

Umar became very angry on hearing these words of the Ansar, and was about to give a reply to this man when Abu Bakr asked him to keep quiet and himself said: "Brothers in Islam, we are the Muhajirin, the first people to enter the fold of Islam, the most respected ones from good homes and families who have sacrificed both in the cause of Islam. And we are the nearest relations of the Prophet of Allah (peace be upon him). We embraced Islam before you did, and were given priority in the Qur'an: 'And the pioneers from the Muhajirin and Ansars and those people who followed them with good deeds . . . .' So we are the Muhajirin and you are the Ansars, our brothers in faith and our partners in land, as well as our supporters against the enemy. Whatever good qualities you have mentioned, you deserve them. And you deserve praise more than all the people of this world. But the Arab people would not recognise your superior position over men from the Quraysh tribe. So the rulers will come from among us and the ministers will be from your-selves."

He then caught Umar and Abu Ubayda bin al-Jarrah by the hand, and said: "I nominate one of these two men for you!"

A man from the *Ansars* got up and said: "O *Ansars*! Don't listen to this speech and that of his companions. They want to take away our share of the administration. And by Allah, we deserve it."

Then came Abu Ubayda, and he said: "O *Ansars*! You were the first among the people to support and protect us. So don't be the first to desert us."

Then a man from the *Ansars* got up and said: "Be careful! Indeed, Muhammad (peace be upon him) is from the *Quraysh*, and his people have priority over others. I am confident that Allah will not take away their right. So we should fear Allah, and not oppse them."

Abu Bakr realised that it was the right moment for him to speak. He got up, and presented the names of two persons from the *Muhajirin* for the position of Caliph: "This is Umar, and this is Abu Ubayda. Take the oath of allegiance to either of them".

Umar said: "By Allah, we can't accept this position before you, because you are the most senior person among the *Muhajirin.* And you were also the Companion of the Prophet (peace be upon him) in the cave. You were the deputy of the Prophet of Allah (peace be upon him) in leading the prayers. And prayers are among the noblest obligations of the faith of the Muslim community. So it is essential that you should be given this position. Show your hand so that we may take the oath of allegiance to you."

Umar and Abu Ubayda were then the first to take the oath of allegiance to Abu Bakr. They were followed by the other people, who took the oath and formally recognised Abu Bakr as the *Khalifa* (the Caliph or successor) of the Prophet of Allah (Peace be upon him).

When the ceremony of the oath of allegiance was over, Abu Bakr went to supervise the funeral of the Prophet of Allah (peace be upon him). Shaqran and Usama bin Zayd were pouring water, and Ali bin Abi Talib was giving him a bath. Three sheets which came from the Yemen were used for the shroud. He was then placed on a coffin carrier and Muslims then came to him in large numbers to invoke Allah's blessings upon him, as he was no longer their leader in prayers. Then came the women followed by the children. The first men to enter the house were Abu Bakr and Umar, together with a few people from the *Muhajirin* and *Ansars*. When the time came to place the Prophet's body (peace be upon him) in the grave, differences arose among the people about the place where the grave should be. Abu Bakr put forward a saying of the Prophet which brought the dispute to an end. He said: "I heard the Prophet of Allah saying: 'No Prophet died without being buried at the place where his death occurred'."

Then came Talha, from the *Ansars*, and he dug the grave for the Prophet of Allah (peace be upon him) and spread the red velvet mantle, which the Prophet (peace be upon him) used to wear, at the bottom of the grave. He then raised the grave a little above the ground.

When the burial ceremony of the Prophet (peace be upon him) was over, Abu Bakr got up, praised Allah the Almighty and delivered his first address to the people as the first Caliph of Islam, outlining the principles of the policy that he would follow: "O people, I have been appointed your chief, and I am not the best of you. Support me if I do good deeds. Remove me if I do anything wrong. Truth is honesty, and lying is dishonesty. The weak among you are strong in my eyes, until I acquire their right for them. And the strong among you are weak before me until I take their right from them, if Allah so wishes. Obey me as long as I obey Allah and His Prophet (peace be upon him). Whenever I disobey Allah and His Propet (peace be upon him), you are not bound to obey me. Get up for your prayers. May Allah show His mercy to you!"

After delivering his address as Caliph in which he explained his rights and obligations to the people, he said that he was a supporter of righteousness wherever it might be, and he invited them to sacrifice their lives in the way of *Jihad* and for the pleasure of Allah. Abu Bakr started to carry out Allah's orders, and paid attention to the duties of the state and its problems. He did his duty with vigour, courage and faith.

Early in the morning on the second day of his Caliphate, Abu Bakr carried rolls of cloth on his shoulder to the market-place. He was going to sell them in order to earn a living. On his way he met Umar bin al-Khattab and Abu Ubayda bin al-Jarrah. Umar asked him: "Where are you going, O Caliph of the Prophet of Allah?"

"I am going to the market", said Abu Bakr.

"You are doing this business even after becoming the head of the Muslim community?"

"How can I feed my family otherwise?"

"Come on with us so that we may arrange something for you".

Abu Bakr went with both of them, and they arranged for him to have two hundred and fifty *dinars* per year and half a goat daily. This, however, was found to be insufficient to meet the needs of his family. The salary was increased to three hundred *dinars* per year and a goat a day. Abu Bakr did not accept this until this was approved by the community.

An interesting story is related about Abu Bakr before his election as the Caliph. He had some goats which he grazed himself. He also used to help the women of his neighbourhood in the meadow by milking their goats. When he became the Caliph, he returned to his house and on the way he heard the women of his neighbourhood saying: "Now he will not milk the goats of our house."

When he heard this, he said: "I give you my word that I will milk your goats. I hope something that has become part of my character will not change."

And he continued to milk their goats.

4

THE CHAMPION

The first setback to Abu Bakr was the great opposition of a large number of the Companions, headed by Umar to sending the Muslim army under the command of Usama bin Zayd to the territory of Qada'a. They opposed his command of the army because he was not yet eighteen years of age.

They chose Umar bin al-Khattab as their representative. He was asked to suggest to Abu Bakr, on their behalf, that either the army should not be sent, or Usama should be dismissed. They wanted to appoint a commander with experience of active service on the battlefield.

Caliph Abu Bakr thought about the objections of these Companions to the despatch of the army under the command of Usama for a long while that day. He then remembered the time when the Prophet (peace be upon him) came to his mosque with his head wrapped up and said: "O People, let the army of Usama go".

He repeated these words three times and continued: "If you condemn his command now, you are also criticising the command of his father previously. And by Allah, he had the qualities required for command! By Allah, his son is one of the most popular men after him!"

When Abu Bakr reported this *Hadith* (saying of the Prophet—peace be upon him), he became determined to send the army of Usama, becaue it was commanded by the Prophet of Allah (peace be upon him), even though it might lead to the loss of his own life. Meanwhile, Umar arrived and asked Abu Bakr not to send the army. Abu Bakr replied: "By Him in whose hands is the life of Abu Bakr, if I would have thought that wild beasts would attack me, I would despatch the army of Usama as ordered by the Prophet (peace be upon him). Even if nobody remained in the city except myself, I would send this army."

When Umar saw that Abu Bakr was determined to despatch the army, he asked him to dismiss Usama and give the command of the army to one of the well-known heroes of Islam, such as Sa'd bin Abi Waqqas or Khalid bin Walid. But Abu Bakr firmly rejected his proposal. The army led by Usama had a great impact at that time, for most of the tribes had given up Islam after the death of the Prophet (peace be upon him) and they had refused to pay *Zakat* (welfare money for the poor). They thought that Islam would come to an end after the Prophet's death. The purpose of despatching the army commanded by Usama was to create fear in the hearts of the tribes who had given up Islam. They said among themselves: "If the Muslims had no power, they would not have sent this army".

This was an example of the wisdom and genius of Abu Bakr at a crucial juncture in the history of Islam.

Later on, Abu Bakr made further preparations for *Jihad* against those people who had given up Allah's faith and launched a full-fledged war against them. They included almost all the tribes of Arabia, except the Quraysh and Thaqif. Abu Bakr saw before his eyes eleven sources of turmoil and anarchy and he wanted to nip the evil in the bud. He assembled the leaders of the Muslim community and appointed them to quell the rebellion against Islam in the eleven different areas as follows:

1. Khalid bin Walid was sent to Talha al-Asadi, with instructions that he should go to Malik bin Nuwaira, after dealing with Talha.

2. Ikrama bin Abi Jihl was sent to fight Musailma al-Kazzab, who had claimed to be a prophet after giving up Islam.

3. al-Muhajir bin Abi Umayya was sent to deal with al-Ansi al-Kazzab, and to fight Kinda in Hadramawt.

4. Khalid bin Sa'id was sent to Syria to quell the rebellion of the leaders of that area.

5. Amr bin al-'As was sent to Qada'a and Wadi'a.

6. Hudhayfa bin Hisn was sent to subdue the people of Daba.

7. Arfaja bin Harthama was sent to Mahra.

8. Shurahbil bin Hasana was sent to help Ikrama bin Abi Jihl, and thence to Qada'a.

9. Ma'n bin Hajiz was sent to Bani Sulaym and the people of Hawazin as well.

10. Suwayd bin Muqrin was sent to Tahama in the Yemen.

11. al-Ala bin al-Hadrami was sent to Bahrain.

The names of the leaders of the eleven armies despatched by Abu Bakr to suppress the rebellion of the tribes who had given up Islam, gives an idea of the great efforts made by him. It was necessary to prepare these armies for the march throughout the country to announce that Islam was strong and alive. These armies achieved victory after very tough battles in which a large number of Companions of the Prophet (peace be upon him) fell as martyrs, including those who remembered the Qur'an by heart. All this sacrifice was made to strengthen Islam and to keep the banner of the faith flying over the various territories.

Abu Bakr made all these great efforts without counting the odds or fearing the difficulties involved in running his mission. He wanted to fight the world that had turned its back on Islam and to bring it back to the right path. One of the narrators of the sayings of the Prophet (peace be upon him) and his Companions, Abu Huraira, has said: "By Allah, beside Whom there is no true God, if there had been no Abu Bakr, Allah would not have been worshipped on this earth."

Abu Huraira had, thus, stated a basic truth.

5

THE VICTOR

When the wars against the rebel tribes had come to an end Abu Bakr turned to the plight of the oppressed masses under the Iranian and the Roman Empires. He called the people to *Jihad*. This means to strive and struggle with one's ability and resources to make God's words supreme. The highest form of *Jihad* is to engage oneself in a battle for the cause of Islam. Since Islam forbids the use of force for converting people to Islam, *Jihad* cannot be a means to conversion. Islam, however, cannot tolerate an ungodly ruler who, denies the basic human and religious rights to his peoples. Muslims have to interfere and correct the situation by negotiations and if necessary by force.

The Qur'an has promised Allah's reward to a Muslim for his participation in *Jihad*. The Prophet Muhammad, in his last years, wanted to send an expedition to Syria to free the peoples from the clutches of the tyrants who were also threatening the very survival of Islam. Abu Bakr had to take up this mission after the prophet. The Muslims had to challenge the formidable oppressors in the neighbouring lands.

Abu Bakr divided his army into four. He made Yazid bin Abi Sufyan Commander of the first army and despatched him to Transjordan. Shurahbil bin Hasana was made Commander of the second army and sent to al-Balqa. Amr bin al-'As was appointed Commander of the third army and was sent to Palestine. Abu Ubayda bin al-Jarrah was made Commander of the fourth army and despatched to Hims (Syria). Abu Ubayda was made Commander-in-Chief of all the armies. Abu Bakr appointed these four Commanders on Thursday, in the beginning of the month of Safar, in the third year of the Caliphate.

The Islamic armies moved in four directions. Amr bin al-'As

camped his army in al-Arabiya, a valley between the Dead Sea and the Gulf of Aqaba. Abu Ubayda reached al-Jabiya, Yazid arrived in al-Balqa and Shurahbil had gone to Transjordan. When the news of these armies reached Heraclius, the Roman Emperor, he said to his people in Jerusalem, where he was staying at that time: "I think we should make peace with the Muslims. If you make peace with them with half of the revenue of Syria, leaving the other half to yourselves, together with the Roman territories, I think it would be better than their taking over the whole of Syria and half of the Roman territories".

They did not listen to his advice. A Roman army was sent to meet each of the Muslim armies, with a much larger number of men and better equipment. The Muslims thought that the division of their army would lead to defeat. They consulted Amr bin al-'As and asked for his opinion in this matter. He said that he thought it would be better for the Muslim armies to join each other: "When our troops gather together, we shall not be dominated because of shortage of numbers. But if we are divided, no army will be able to meet the large number of the enemy".

Then they asked for the opinion of their Caliph, Abu Bakr. He advised the four Muslim armies to fight the enemy at Yarmuk together. Abu Bakr, therefore, gave greater importance to the conquest of Syria than the conquest of Iraq. He ordered Khalid bin Walid, who was in Iraq at that time, to go to Yarmuk with half his army, and al-Muthanna bin Haritha al-Shaybani to fight the Persians with the remaining half of the Muslim army. The Muslim army reached Yarmuk as ordered by the Caliph and the Roman army took up positions in front of them.

When Khalid Bin Walid arrived in Yarmuk, he found the four Muslim armies fighting the Romans under their Commanders.

He joined these armies together, and made them one army. He divided the command of the army between himself and the four Commanders, each taking his duty in turn daily. The two armies fought courageously.

The Muslim army achieved victory after a decisive battle. They conquered the territories of Syria and established an Islamic order there. Syria continues to be a Muslim country down to the present day.

When the Muslim army was fighting the Romans in Yarmuk al-Muthanna bin Haritha al-Shaybani was fighting the Persians in Iraq. He was a strong young man and a very good Muslim.

He had embraced Islam in the tenth year of the *Hijra*. He led a small army and successfully attacked the territories of Iraq. When Abu Bakr received the news of his victories, he was surprised and said: "Who is this man the stories of whose victories have reached us?"

Qays Bin Asim told him: "He is not an unknown person. His ancestors are also not unknown. The number of his family is not small, and his heroic deeds are not of a low order. This man is al-Muthanna bin Haritha al-Shaybani".

Later on al-Muthanna came to see Abu Bakr, and said to him: "O Caliph of the Prophet of Allah (peace be upon him)! Appoint me the Commander of good Muslims, and I will fight the Persians." Abu Bakr appointed him as Commander. Afterwards, he sent Khalid bin Walid to Iraq. Thus Abu Bakr, the first Caliph, became the benefactor of Iraq and Syria.

One day, Umar bin al-Khattab was reciting some verses from the Qur'an. After finishing his recitation, he pondered over the meaning of the Qur'an and admired its eloquence. Suddenly, his chain of thought was disturbed, and it came to his mind that the Prophet (peace be upon him) was dead, and the Qur'an had not yet been reduced to writing in the form of a book. Also a large number of men who knew the Qur'an by heart had fallen as martyrs in the Battle of Yamama. This was fought against Musaylma al-Kazzab, who had given up Islam and claimed to be a prophet.

So Umar went to see Abu Bakr, and said: "Abu Bakr, I have come to see you about a very important matter."

"It will be important, if Allah wills it", replied Abu Bakr.

Umar then explained: "Too many people fell as martyrs in the Battle of Yamama. I am afraid that if we continue to lose in battles the men who know the Qur'an by heart, a large part of the Qur'an may be lost. I am of the opinion that the Qur'an must be collected and put into writing as a book."

Abu Bakr looked at Umar with awe and surprise and said: "How can I do something which the Propet (peace be upon him) did not do?"

"By Allah, it will be necessary, Abu Bakr!", said Umar, who kept on insisting as to the importance of the matter. Finally, both of them agreed that the Qur'an must be collected in a book-form.

Abu Bakr sent for Zayd bin Thabit who used to write the verses of the Qur'an for the Prophet of Allah (peace be upon him) as and when they were revealed to him. Abu Bakr explained to him what Umar had said, and then told him: "You are a wise young man. We have nothing to say against you. You used to write the revelation for the Prophet of Allah (peace be upon him). Now you should search for the Qur'an and collect it together." Zayd said of this mission: "By Allah, if I had been asked to move a mountain, it would not have been such a heavy responsibility for me as the collection of the Qur'an".

Zayd looked at Abu Bakr and Umar and said to them: "How can I do something that was not done by the Prophet of Allah (peace be upon him)?"

Abu Bakr replied: "By Allah, it will be of great benefit".

One of the earliest copies of the Qur'an in Topkapi Museum, Istanbul, Turkey.

Abu Bakr explained to Zayd bin Thabit the importance of the mission, until he was convinced. Zayd then started collecting the Qur'an from pieces of skin, slabs of stone and blades of wood on which it was written as well as from the memory of the people. Allah helped him in this great task.

There is no need to explain here the importance of the collection of the Qur'an. If Allah had not taken the responsibility of preserving it, as mentioned in the Qur'an: "We have indeed revealed this Book of wisdom, and indeed We shall preserve it" and if Abu Bakr had not started its collection, the story-tellers and fabricators, as well as the hypocrites, would have tried to tamper with the Qur'an by changing some verses of it. If the *Imams* (leading Muslim scholars) of *Hadith* (sayings of the Prophet—peace be upon him) and *Huffaz* (Muslims who remember the Qur'an by heart) had not collected the sayings of the Prophet (peace be upon him) and had not separated the correct sayings from the incorrect ones in the latter half of the second century of the Hijra, the *Sunna* (tradition) of the Prophet (peace be upon him) would have been lost.

We are grateful to Imam Malik, Imam Bukhari, Imam Muslim and others who worked devotedly collecting and selecting the sayings of the Prophet (peace be upon him) for the coming generations. We are also grateful to the Caliph Abu Bakr as-Siddiq for collecting the Qur'an. May Allah reward them adequately for their sincere services to Islam.

6

THE ADMINISTRATOR

Abu Bakr remained in his office as the Caliph of the Muslim community for two years, three months and ten days. He ruled the Islamic *Umma* (Muslim community in the world) in the best manner. This was the first Islamic Government. We thought that it would be better to mention the policies and principles of the first Islamic Government in this last chapter, before mentioning Abu Bakr's death. We shall make a brief reference to the ministers and officials of Abu Bakr's government, which controlled vast territories. In this way, we may be able to show the difference between the government of those people who rule according to Allah's book and the law of the heavens and the government of those who rule according to man-made laws. We shall start mentioning Abu Bakr first of all.

Abu Bakr was an extremely pious and righteous man. Signs of his strong faith and reliance on Allah rather than on any worldly source were clearly visible in his personality. We have read in some of his old biographies a strange story which reveals his condition of poverty in the last days of the Prophet (peace be upon him). And it was the same man who possessed a capital of about forty thousand *dirhams* when he embraced Islam.

Here is a summary of the story. One day, Abu Bakr was sitting in the company of the Prophet (peace be upon him), and he was wearing an old gown, torn in a few places and showing his chest. Jibrail, the Angel who brought the revelations, came to the Prophet (peace be upon him) and saw the condition of Abu Bakr. The Angel said to the Prophet (peace be upon him): "Allah greets you, and asks you to tell Abu Bakr that Allah gives His blessing to him and asks: 'Is he pleased with Me in his poverty or not?' "

The Prophet (peace be upon him) then addressed Abu Bakr and said: "O Abu Bakr, Allah greets you and asks you whether you are pleased with Him or not?"

Then Abu Bakr replied: "I am pleased with my Lord. I am pleased with my Lord. I desire that He may be pleased with me".

One of the interesting stories told about Abu Bakr when he was Caliph refers to his concern for his subject's welfare. This concern was so great that it sometimes kept him awake at night. Umar bin al-Khattab used to go to the house of an old woman to help her with her household chores. One day, when Umar went to ask her what she needed doing, she told him that a man had come before his arrival and had done all the necessary jobs. Umar continued to visit the old woman for several days. One day, he went to her house early and while he was standing at her door, he saw a man, whose face was covered, going out of her house into the street. Umar followed him quickly until he caught up with him. The man removed the cover from his face and Umar saw that he was Abu Bakr as-Siddiq, the Caliph. Umar said to him: "I was sure that it was you. I knew that no one else would have a lead over me except you."

Such were the early rulers of Islam. They kept awake at night thinking of the welfare of their subjects and vied with each other in serving them.

Now we shall mention the ministers of the first Islamic government. The well-known Companions of the Prophet, Abu Ubayda bin al-Jarrah, was the Minister of Finance. The Minister of Finance in those days looked after everything that was related to the revenues of the State, such as *Kharaj* (land tax), *Ushr* (tithe or one-tenth of the agricultural revenue tax), *Khums* (income tax) and *Jizya* (the tax taken from non-Muslim subjects for their protection by the State). The Minister was also responsible for the welfare of the Muslim community, the equipment of the troops, monthly convoys for the troops and other important matters.

The Ministry of Justice was under Umar bin al-Khattab. It was a strange coincidence that after Umar became the Minister of Justice, he had no dispute to settle between two men fighting over something. This fact shows the state of peace and satisfaction among the people and the spirit of brotherhood that dominated them at that time. The truth is that the social conditions of the Muslim community during the period of the first Islamic government were the best that one could desire. The Muslims were blessed with the spirit of justice and equality, brotherhood and sacrifice: always the results of a people carrying out the commands of Allah. If we look at our present age,

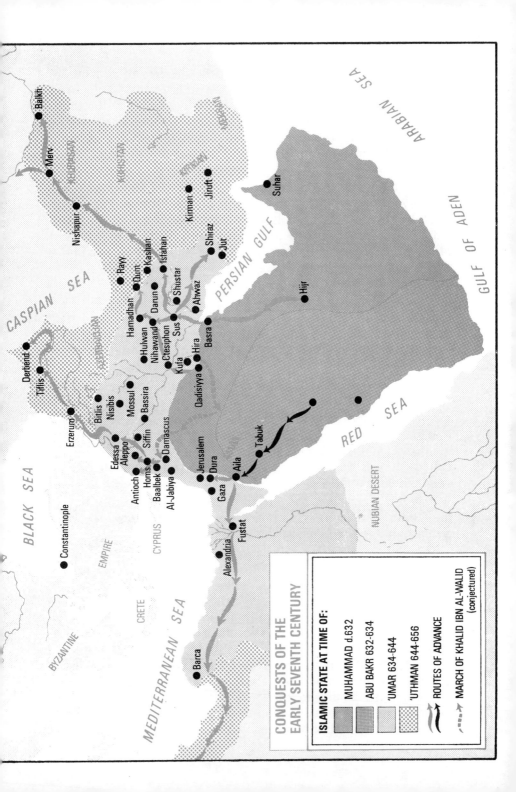

CONQUESTS OF THE
EARLY SEVENTH CENTURY

ISLAMIC STATE AT TIME OF:

MUHAMMAD d.632

ABU BAKR 632-634

'UMAR 634-644

'UTHMAN 644-656

ROUTES OF ADVANCE

MARCH OF KHALID IBN AL-WALID
(conjectured)

ARABIAN SEA

GULF OF ADEN

PERSIAN GULF

CASPIAN SEA

BLACK SEA

MEDITERRANEAN SEA

RED SEA

NUBIAN DESERT

BYZANTINE EMPIRE

CRETE

CYPRUS

Balkh

Merv

Nishapur

KHURASAN

Rayy

Hamadhan

Qum

Kashan

Isfahan

Darun

Shustar

Shiraz

Jur

Kirman

Jiroft

Suhar

Hijr

Ahwaz

Sus

Basra

Nihawand

Ctesiphon

Hira

Huiwan

Kufa

Qadisiyya

Derbent

Tiflis

Erzerum

Bitlis

Nisibis

Mossul

Bassira

ADHARBAYJAN

Edessa

Aleppo

Antioch

Homs

Siffin

Damascus

Baalbek

Al-Jabiya

Jerusalem

Dura

Gaza

Aila

Tabuk

Fustat

Alexandria

Barca

Constantinople

the daily newspapers are full of reports of crime of all kinds at every hour and in every place. In the time of the Caliph Abu Bakr as-Siddiq, those entrusted with the leadership of the Muslims ruled according to the laws revealed by Allah. It shows us the great difference between the laws and regulations of Islam and man-made laws of the past and present.

There were ten provinces in Arabia at the time of Abu Bakr. Each of them had a governor. The Governor of Makka was Itab bin Usyad, one of the Companions of the Prophet (peace be upon him) who embraced Islam on the day of the conquest of Makka. The Prophet (peace be upon him) made him Governor of Makka when he was twenty years of age, and he became a pious and learned man. It was a strange coincidence that he and Abu Bakr died on the same day.

Uthman bin al-'As was the governor of Taif. The Prophet (peace be upon him) appointed him Governor of Taif, and Abu Bakr maintained him in that position. He reported nine *Ahadith* (sayings of the Prophet). Imam Muslim has reported three of them. He died during the Caliphate of Mu'awiya.

The Governor of San'a was al-Muhajir bin Abi Umayya. He was a brother of Umm Salma, one of the wives of the Prophet.

The Governor of Hadramaut was Ziyad bin Labid, a citizen of Madina. After embracing Islam, he lived with the Prophet in Makka and later migrated to Madina. He was, therefore, called *Muhajir Ansari*, and was one of those Companions who spent their whole lives with the Prophet (peace be upon him).

Yala bin Munya was the Governor of Khaulan, a great tribe of the Yemen. He embraced Islam on the day Makka was conquered, and fell as a martyr at the Battle of Siffin.

The Governor of Zubaida, a valley in the Yemen, was Abu Musa al-Ashari. He met the Prophet (peace be upon him) in Makka before his migration to Madina, and embraced Islam. He migrated to Abyssinia (Ethiopia) first and later to Madina. The Prophet (peace be upon him) appointed him Governor of Zabida and Aden, as well as the coast of the Yemen. He died in Makka in 50 A.H./670 C.E.

Muaz bin Jabal was the Governor of al-Janad. He was a scholar of *Fiqh* (Islamic Jurisprudence) and a pious man. When he embraced Islam together with seventy *Ansars*, he was eighteen years of age. He died of plague in Syria.

The Governor of Bahrain was al-Ala bin Hadrami. The Prophet

(peace be upon him) made him Governor of Bahrain. Abu Bakr confirmed his appointment. He was one of those people whose prayers were readily accepted by Allah. He had a great influence in the battle against those who had given up Islam near Bahrain. He died as a Governor in 14 A.H./635 C.E.

Jarir bin Abdullah was the Governor of Najran. He had met the Prophet (peace be upon him) in the month of Ramadan, in the year of 10 A.H./631 C.E. and embraced Islam then.

Abdullah bin Thaub Abu Muslim al-Khawlani was the Governor of Jursh in the Yemen. He was one of the great Tabi'in (companions of the Companions of the Prophet—peace be upon him) and a learned and pious man. He embraced Islam during the lifetime of the Prophet (peace be upon him) and died in 20 A.H./640 C.E.

These were the ministers and leading officials of Abu Bakr's Government and some of the chosen Companions of the Prophet (peace be upon him).

The main reason for the grandeur and power of the Muslim *Umma* (Muslim community in the world) was the way of life adopted by these ministers. They applied the laws of Islam to themselves, and followed its teachings word by word and in the true spirit. They ruled the people with justice. Allah blessed their efforts with success.

Muslims believe that the welfare of the *Umma* lies in the reform of its rulers and *Ulama* (scholars of Islam), as the Prophet (peace be upon him) had said: "When the two groups of my *Umma* (the rulers and the *Ulama*) are reformed the entire community will be reformed, and when they become corrupt the entire community will become corrupt."

The Prophet (peace be upon him) in this saying has explained the disease. Allah has shown its remedy in His Book, the Qur'an. And there is no remedy except to return to living according to the laws revealed by Allah.

During the latter days of the first government, on a Monday, the seventh of Jamadi-al-Thani, the thirteenth year of the *Hijra,* Abu Bakr entered the *hammam* (bathroom) to take a bath. It was a cold day, and when he came out, he felt a slight chill, which turned into a fever. As he could not go to prayers, he ordered Umar to lead the prayers.

When he saw his illness getting worse, he thought about

appointing a successor so that there might be no dispute over succession as had happened after the death of the Prophet (peace be upon him). He sent for Abdur Rahman bin Awf, and asked him: "Tell me what is your opinion about Umar?"

He replied: "O Caliph of the Prophet of Allah, he is the most superior of all men, but he is harsh".

Abu Bakr said: "This is so because he finds me tender-hearted. If he comes to power, he will lose most of his harshness". Then he sent for Uthman bin Affan, Usyd bin Hadir, Sa'id bin Zayd, and some of the *Muhajirin* and *Ansars*, and asked them their opinion. All of them praised Umar.

Then Abu Bakr sent for his secretary, Uthman bin Affan, and said to him: "Write in the name of Allah, the Beneficent, the Merciful. This is what Abu Bakr bin Abi Qahafa promised to the Muslim community". Then he went into a coma.

Uthman bin Affan wrote himself: "And I hereby appoint Umar bin al-Khattab as my successor for you. And I did not find anyone better than him".

Later Abu Bakr regained consciousness and said: "I saw you were afraid that if I died in coma, differences would arise among the people".

"Yes".

"May Allah reward you on behalf of Islam and its people".

Then Abu Bakr read what Uthman had written. He ordered the will to be written and sealed. Uthman then went out with the sealed Will, and the people took the oath of allegiance to Umar bin al-Khattab.

After a few days, Abu Bakr's fever became high, and he died on Monday, 22nd Jamadi-al-Thani, 13 A.H./634 C.E. The funeral prayers were led by Umar bin al-Khattab. Four men recited *takbir* (Allah Akbar) in the mosque of the Prophet (peace be upon him), between his grave and the pulpit. And then Abu Bakr was buried near the Prophet (peace be upon him).